Annabel Karmel's
FUN FAST &EASY
CHILDREN'S COOKBOOK

Annabel Karmel's FUN FAST & EASY CHILDREN'S COOKBOOK

Illustrated by Bryony Clarkson

WELBECK

Published in 2021 by Welbeck
Part of Welbeck Publishing Group
20 Mortimer Street, London W1T 3JW

A CIP catalogue record for this book
is available from the British Library.

ISBN 978 1 78739 816 0

Printed in Heshan, China

10 9 8 7 6 5 4 3 2 1

Design and Art Direction: Smith & Gilmour
Editor: Jo Roberts-Miller
Illustrator: Bryony Clarkson
Food photography: Ant Duncan
and Jamie Orlando-Smith pp. 51, 57, 83, 89 and 97
Endpaper photography: Emma Tunbridge
Food stylists: Holly Cowgill and Becci Woods
Props stylist: Tamsin Weston
Models: Iris, Ray, Ace, Chiara, Hugo, Isla,
Vicky, Havanna, Hattie and Alma.
Design Managers: Emily Clarke, Margaret Hope
Editorial Manager: Joff Brown
Production: Melanie Robertson

Contents

Let's get started!

A little message for grown-ups

Welcome to my fun kids' cookbook! It's designed so that budding chefs and bakers will have a blast in the kitchen – and learn plenty of new skills along the way.

Aprons at the ready! My step-by-step guide, packed with simple recipes, will help your kitchen helpers feel like cooking heroes! From power-packed breakfasts and superhero snacks, to family dinner winners and special treats, it's time for your mini cooks to take centre stage.

There are boundless benefits to getting even the youngest of children cooking with you. From simple tasks like mixing, mashing and rolling, to weighing, counting and grating, inviting kids to explore in the kitchen engages all of their senses and encourages learning.

Some of my happiest memories are of my children cooking and baking. As soon as they were old enough to stand on a chair beside me, I'd get them to help out. In fact, by the time my three children were 4, 6 and 7, they would be cooking dinner for the family every Friday (sometimes with a bit of a helping hand). They'd pick a recipe, prepare it and then serve it up in the 'Karmel restaurant'! They loved eating what they had prepared, and it was a great way to get them trying different foods.

Cooking parties were also a hit in our home. Whether it was a birthday, sleepover or after-school playdate, my kids and their friends loved being in charge of making a fun spread!

Every recipe in this colourful cookbook has been designed for children and grown-ups to cook together. As little chefs grow in skill and confidence, they will be able to take the lead on many of the recipe steps. It's important to keep a close eye on children in the kitchen at all times, and be especially careful of anything hot or sharp.

You'll find helpful tips, twists and swaps on lots of the recipes, so have fun and experiment. Here's to making memories in the kitchen!

Annabel's kitchen rules

Do I hear little tummies rumbling? Are you ready to transform into a crafty chef or brilliant baker? Here are some handy tips to help you get started and have fun in the kitchen.

- Remember to wash your hands so that they are squeaky clean. Cooking can get messy, so pop on an apron and tie your hair back if it's long.

- Before you start, read the recipe (or get a grown-up to read it for you), to make sure you have everything you need. I often find it helpful to weigh, measure and count out ingredients at the beginning so they are ready to use.

- Be careful of anything hot. Things that have just come out of the oven or off the hob will take a while to cool down, so don't touch!

- Always wash fruit and vegetables before you cook or eat them.

- All cutting, slicing and chopping with sharp knives should be done by a grown-up or under adult supervision.

- Not all uncooked ingredients or mixtures are safe to eat, so check with a grown-up first. We don't want any upset tummies!

- If you are cooking for someone with allergies, make sure the ingredients are safe – you'll find out more about this on the next pages.

Kitchen equipment

Chefs – it's time to pick up your tools! Just like any professional, you'll need some basic equipment to get your cook on!

★ Wooden spoons and plastic spatulas

★ Measuring spoons

★ Chopping board and special nylon or plastic children's knife

★ Mixing bowls – small and large

★ Colander and/or sieve

★ Saucepans – small and large

★ Frying pans (non-stick is best and a wok is also useful for stir-frying)

★ Electric whisk – makes beating the butter and sugar for cookies, cupcakes and icing much quicker

★ Food processor or hand blender – for speedy chopping and blending!

★ Fun-shaped cookie cutters

★ Baking trays and muffin tins – non-stick ones are best

★ Non-stick paper and muffin paper cases

Annabel's GREAT top tips

G **Get** all your ingredients ready before you begin.

R **Read** the recipe through before you start.

E **Enjoy** yourself – cooking is meant to be FUN (and YUM)!

A **Always** tell a grown-up what you are doing and get them to help.

T **Tidy** up before munching away on your tasty creations.

Be allergy aware!

If you have a food allergy, or you are cooking for someone with a dietary requirement, my recipes can easily be adapted, and here are a few helpful tips.

★ **Dairy free**
Try soy or coconut yoghurt instead of dairy yoghurt; oat or almond milk instead of cow's milk; olive oil instead of butter for frying; soft dairy-free spread instead of butter for buttercream icing; and vegan cheeses for Cheddar, Parmesan and cream cheese.

★ **Gluten free**
Use gluten free varieties of flour, baking powder and pasta. Also try rice, oats, quinoa and buckwheat (nothing to do with wheat despite the name!), which are all naturally gluten free.

★ **Egg free**
Whether you don't eat eggs by choice or because you have an allergy, check out my website for my egg substitution guide for baking and cooking (www.annabelkarmel.com).

Simple swaps

If you don't eat meat or fish, then most of my recipes are easy to turn into veggie or vegan versions. Add your own spin on recipes and try swapping chicken, beef or prawns for halloumi, tofu and lentils, or your family's favourite plant-based mince.

KEY TO SYMBOLS

gluten free — gluten free

egg free — egg free

dairy free — dairy free if made with non-dairy milk where required

veggie — veggie

vegan — vegan

freeze — suitable for freezing (ready to enjoy again another day!)

BREAKFAST

RAINBOW
Yoghurt Bowl

20g cream cheese

200g Greek yoghurt

150g tinned peaches, chopped, or 1 fresh peach, peeled, destoned and chopped

25g raspberries, halved

TO DECORATE

8-10 blueberries

2 strawberries, sliced

1 kiwi, peeled and sliced

1 satsuma, peeled

Breakfasts are better with rainbows! Here is a feast for the eyes and the tummy. Packed with colourful fruits, this bowl of goodness will help you start the day with a smile, and help towards your 5-a-day. Hooray!

1 Mix the cream cheese, yoghurt and half the peaches in a small bowl.

2 Place the remaining peaches in the base of a small breakfast bowl and add the halved raspberries.

3 Spoon the yoghurt mixture on top of the raspberries.

4 Use the blueberries, strawberries, kiwi and satsuma to decorate the top of the yoghurt.

Why not try this?
Make a rainbow, flower, owl or rocket with the fruit. Try a new creation each time.

gluten free

vegan

veggie

egg free

serves 1

OWL PORRIDGE

Have a hoot making this wise little owl. A warm bowl of porridge is the perfect way to start the day and it will keep you feeling full all morning. This simple recipe comes with a twit twoo just for you.

1 Measure the oats and milk into a saucepan. Place over a medium heat and bring to the boil, stirring all the time.

2 Add the banana, vanilla extract and coconut, if using, and continue to stir until the porridge has thickened and the oats are soft. This should take about 5 minutes.

3 Spoon into a bowl and use the fruit to decorate the top.

 45g porridge oats

 275ml milk of choice

1 small banana, mashed

 ½ tsp vanilla extract

 2 tsp unsweetened desiccated coconut (optional)

TO DECORATE

 4 strawberries, sliced

 ½ banana, sliced

 2 blueberries

½ mango, sliced

Why not try this?
To make the owl use strawberries for wings, banana slices for the eyes and body, blueberries for the eyeballs and mango for the nose, eyebrows and feet.

veggie

gluten free

vegan

dairy free

egg free

makes 8 portions

GO-GO GRANOLA

175g rolled oats

70g pecans, chopped

20g unsweetened desiccated coconut

50g soft brown sugar

¼ tsp salt

2 tbsp sunflower oil

4 tbsp maple syrup

50g raisins

My Go-Go Granola will have your engines revved and ready for the day! Oats are packed with crunchy goodness, so why not have a second helping after school, too? It's also a good recipe for breakfast in bed on Mother's Day.

1 Preheat the oven to 170°C/Fan 150°C/Gas 3 and line a baking tray with non-stick paper.

2 Tip the oats, pecans, coconut, sugar and salt into a large bowl and mix together well.

3 Measure the oil and maple syrup into a small bowl and whisk together.

4 Pour the oil mixture over the oat mixture and use your hands to scrunch everything together.

5 Spread the granola out evenly on the prepared tray and bake in the oven for 40 minutes, turning with a spatula every 10 minutes, until lightly golden.

6 Remove from the oven and transfer to a bowl. Stir in the raisins and leave to cool.

7 Tip into an airtight container until ready to serve.

Why not try this?
Measure out one portion of granola and add 100g yoghurt and a handful of berry fruits to create a brilliant breakfast bowl.

dairy free

veggie

serves 1

1 mini wholemeal pitta

1 large egg

2 tsp sunflower oil

2 thin slices black olive

6 chives

Why not try this?

I've shown you how to turn your egg into a bunny, but what about making dogs, cats, or other animals instead?

Sunny-Side-Up BUNNIES

Here's an idea to get you and your breakfast guests hopping to the table! Eggs are super nutritious and scrummy to eat runny – perfect for dipping those bunny ears. This is also a great opportunity to practise your egg cracking skills.

1 Slice the pitta in half through the middle and lightly toast in a toaster. Cut out two ear shapes and set aside.

2 Carefully crack the egg into a small bowl.

3 Place the oil in a small non-stick frying pan over a medium heat. Carefully tip the egg into the pan and let it cook for 3–4 minutes, until the whites are completely set but the yolk is still soft.

4 Remove and place sunny-side-up on a plate.

5 Add the pitta slices for ears, olives for eyes and chives for whiskers.

6 Your bunny is ready to hop to the table!

Delicious Dairy

Milk, cream, butter, cheese and yoghurt are dairy products, which means they come from animals like cows, sheep or goats. Most of the milk we drink comes from cows, and it's perfect for a healthy start to your day!

Did you know?
Dairy cows drink a bathtub full of water and need nearly 50 kilos of food each day – that's like eating 300 peanut butter sandwiches!

HEALTHY BONES

Dairy foods are a super source of calcium – a nutrient we all need for strong bones and teeth.

YOGHURT

Yoghurt is filled with goodness and makes for the perfect pud – especially when mixed with your favourite fruits.

Which of these will you dunk into your yoghurt pot?

Did you eat something spicy?
Milk is better for cooling your mouth than water as it cleanses your taste buds!

CHEESE

Cheese is a food made from milk, and thousands of different cheeses are produced and eaten all over the world. Each one has a unique flavour, texture and appearance.

Did you know?

Mice actually don't like cheese. Given the choice, they prefer sweets and carbs! Sure, they'll eat cheese if it's the only thing going, but they don't particularly love it.

BUTTER IT UP!

Did you know you can make delicious whipped cream and butter yourself? All it takes is some double cream, a whisk and a lot of whipping!

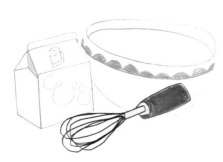

1 Use a whisk to whip double cream in a bowl.

2 Stop whipping when soft peaks form – congrats, you've made whipped cream. It's as easy as that!

3 Fancy transforming that cream into butter? Keep whipping until it gets even thicker and the liquid part (called buttermilk) separates, and lumps of butter start to form. Pour off the buttermilk, et voilà, scoop out your delicious homemade butter. And just in time for lunch!

Did you know?

You can also beat flavours into butter! Try adding a little chopped garlic and parsley, or another herb. Or try grated Parmesan, basil and sundried tomato.

EGGY RAISIN BREAD

 1 egg

 1 slice raisin bread, cut into 3 fingers

 a knob of butter or splash of sunflower oil

This recipe is a real weekend winner!

1 Crack the egg into a shallow bowl. Beat with a fork to mix the yolk into the white.

2 Dip the raisin bread fingers into the egg so that they are coated completely. Leave them to soak until all the egg has been absorbed.

3 Meanwhile, melt the butter or heat the oil in a small frying pan over a medium heat.

4 Add the fingers to the pan and fry for 2 minutes on each side, until golden.

5 Serve with berries.

Why not try this?

At Christmas, you could cook multiple slices of eggy bread and arrange them into the shape of a tree. Decorate your tree with blueberry baubles and top it with a raspberry star for a really festive feast.

veggie · **dairy free** · **makes 8 large or 14 small** · **freeze**

PERFECT PANCAKES

 200g self-raising flour

 1 tbsp caster sugar

 3 eggs

 175ml milk of choice

1 tsp sunflower oil

honey, to drizzle

TO DECORATE

 2 strawberries

 handful of blueberries

It's time to practise your whisking and flipping skills with my perfect pancakes! Here's a little tip – to make your pancake batter nice and smooth, add the liquid slowly and whisk as you go.

1 Measure the flour and sugar into a mixing bowl.

2 Make a well in the centre and crack in the eggs.

3 Carefully pour half the milk into the bowl and whisk everything together until you have a smooth batter. Slowly add the rest of the milk, whisking as you go.

4 Place the oil in a frying pan over a medium heat. Add 2 large spoonfuls of the mixture and fry for 1–2 minutes on each side, until lightly golden and cooked through.

5 Remove from the pan and place on a plate. Cover with a tea towel to keep warm while you make the rest. Continue until all the batter has been used up.

6 Serve with the fruit and honey drizzled over them.

Why not try this?
Line up the pancakes to make a breakfast caterpillar – use slices of strawberry for the legs and mouth, and blueberries for eyes.

2 eggs

1 tbsp milk
of choice

a knob of butter
or splash of
sunflower oil

My first OMELETTE

Eggs at the ready, it's omelettes for brekkie! I'm going to help you master the art of omelette making with my simple recipe and choice of fillings. Add the eggs-factor to your breakfast with this nutritious dish!

1 Carefully crack the eggs into a small bowl. Add the milk, lightly season and beat with a fork.

2 Melt the butter or heat the oil in a small omelette pan over a medium heat.

3 Add the egg mixture and gently pull in the sides of the omelette with a wooden spoon or spatula as it starts to set.

4 Once most of the egg has set, add your choice of filling (if you haven't added it already – see below). Flip one third of the omelette over, then flip over the other side and serve.

CHEESE AND HERB

Add 20g grated Cheddar, 1 tsp chopped fresh basil and 1 tsp snipped fresh chives to the egg mixture in the bowl, then cook as above.

CHERRY TOMATO

Add 3 halved cherry tomatoes and 1 trimmed and finely sliced spring onion to the pan once most of the egg has set.

HAM

Cut 1 slice of ham into strips then add to the pan once most of the egg has set.

Lunch

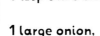
1 tbsp olive oil

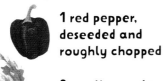
1 large onion, peeled and roughly chopped

1 stick celery, roughly chopped

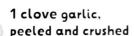
1 red pepper, deseeded and roughly chopped

2 small carrots, peeled and thinly sliced

100g butternut squash, peeled and diced

1 clove garlic, peeled and crushed

1 tsp chopped fresh thyme

1 tbsp tomato purée

1 x 400g tin chopped tomatoes

450ml vegetable or chicken stock

2 tbsp chopped fresh basil (optional)

2 tbsp crème fraîche

pinch of sugar

Tasty TOMATO and VEGETABLE SOUP

Did you know that superheroes love soup? They'd especially love this recipe as it's supercharged with veggies and blended into a smooth bowl of power-packed goodness!

1 Place the oil in a saucepan over a medium heat. Add all the fresh vegetables and fry for 5 minutes, stirring occasionally.

2 Add the garlic, thyme and tomato purée and fry for a further 10 seconds.

3 Tip in the chopped tomatoes and stock, season with salt and pepper and bring to a boil. Reduce the heat, cover with a lid and simmer for 15–20 minutes, or until all the vegetables are tender.

4 Remove from the heat and stir in the basil, if using, and crème fraîche. Add the sugar and blend until smooth using a stick blender.

5 Serve in deep bowls. Season to taste.

Why not try this?

Can you create your own superhero? Use grated cheese for the mask, with circles of toast and black olives for eyes.

Little Italy
BRUSCHETTA

½ loaf ciabatta bread, cut into 6 slices

3 tbsp olive oil

200g cherry tomatoes, diced

75g fresh mozzarella, diced

2 tbsp chopped fresh basil

½ clove garlic, peeled and crushed

A little like 'toast pizza', this is an easy-peasy Italian-inspired recipe you'll love to make and share. The best thing is that you can make it as a starter, brunch or lunch. Tomatoes are packed with goodness too, so get dicing and sprinkling!

1 Preheat the grill to high.

2 Brush the ciabatta slices with 2 tablespoons of the olive oil. Place the slices of bread under the grill and toast for 2–3 minutes on each side. Alternatively, heat a ridged griddle pan until very hot (take care not to touch) and place the ciabatta in the pan on a diagonal. Cook for 2 minutes on each side, until golden with charred lines across each slice.

3 Meanwhile, mix the tomatoes, mozzarella, basil, remaining olive oil and garlic together in a small bowl. Season with salt and pepper.

4 Spoon the tomato mixture onto the slices to serve.

Why not try this?

Turn these ingredients into a delicious salad! Cut the ciabatta into cubes and coat with oil before toasting to make delicious croûtons. Serve them on a bed of sliced tomato, crunchy lettuce and soft mozzarella.

Glorious Grains

Many yummy foods fall into the grain category, including bread, pasta, rice and cereal. And there is a particular type of healthy grain that will help supercharge your body – WHOLE grain! Brown rice, wholewheat pasta and wholegrain bread are jam-packed with fibre, iron and many vitamins and nutrients. Give them a whirl!

BREAD

Bread is made from grains that have been ground into flour. The flour is mixed with yeast, water and salt then kneaded into a dough and baked.

★ Yeast is the magic agent that makes the dough rise.

★ Bread can also be flat – like pitta bread, tortillas and pizza dough bases.

GOLDEN GRAINS

Quinoa, pronounced 'keen-wa', is a whole grain that was highly prized by the ancient Incas – they called it 'gold of the Incas'.

RICE, PASTA AND NOODLES

What do rice, pasta and noodles have in common? They are a good source of carbohydrates to help fuel your body, providing a slow release of energy for fun, play and learning!

Did you know that rice is the main food for about half of the world's population? Pasta is super popular too, with over 600 types to choose from. Which shapes do you have in your kitchen cupboard?

Penne

Conchiglie

Macaroni

Fusilli

Farfalle

Did you know?
In Japan, slurping loudly while eating your noodles shows that you are enjoying the delicious meal made by your host!

ANNABEL'S RULES

When cooking, make sure a grown-up is there to help you. The kernels need to get SO HOT that they explode or POP, so never leave your corn unattended.

Although you can microwave popcorn, it's extra fun to watch the kernels pop in a pan. You might like to eat the popcorn plain or try with a little melted butter or sprinkling of cinnamon as a treat.

POP IT!

Want to see how corn pops? Homemade popcorn is easy to make using dried corn kernels, and you can add your own toppings!

1. Heat oil in a heavy saucepan. Drop 3-4 kernels into the oil and wait until they pop. This means it's hot enough!

2. When hot add the rest of the kernels and jiggle around so they are covered in oil.

3. Cover the pan TIGHTLY. Listen for POPPING and remove from the heat when the popping stops.

Super POT NOODLES

 75g medium egg noodles

 1 tsp cornflour

2 tsp sunflower oil

 3 spring onions, sliced

 1 small carrot, peeled and grated

 2 tbsp frozen sweetcorn

 25g frozen peas

 100g cooked chicken, cut into chunks

150ml hot chicken stock

1½ tbsp soy sauce

pinch of sugar

 60g beansprouts

We all love oodles of noodles, so this is a dinner winner! Did you know that the very first noodle was made 4,000 years ago in China?

1 Cook the noodles according to the packet instructions. Drain, then run under cold water to stop them cooking. Set aside.

2 Combine the cornflour with 1 tablespoon of cold water in a small bowl.

3 Place the oil in a non-stick frying pan over a medium heat. Add the spring onions and carrot, and fry for 1 minute, stirring regularly.

4 Add the cooked noodles, sweetcorn, peas and chicken and stir-fry for a few seconds.

5 Pour in the hot stock, then add the soy sauce and sugar.

6 Add the cornflour mixture and beansprouts to the pan and toss over the heat until the sauce has thickened.

7 Divide between two deep bowls and serve with chopsticks and spoons.

Why not try this?
Try eating your noodles with chopsticks. It's super fun and, with a little practice, you'll be a champion in no time!

MIGHTY Muffins Trio

225g self-raising flour

1 tsp baking powder

50g Parmesan, grated

75g Cheddar, grated

2 eggs

175ml milk

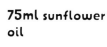
75ml sunflower oil

It's great to mix things up, especially when it comes to cooking, so here are three tasty twists on my muffin recipe. These are super yummy eaten hot, but also make a fun and healthy lunchbox treat. Or why not bake a batch and share them with your friends?

1 Preheat the oven to 200°C/Fan 180°C/Gas 6 and line a 12-hole muffin tin with paper cases.

2 To make the basic mixture, combine the flour, baking powder, cheeses and a pinch of salt in a large bowl.

3 Beat the eggs, milk and oil in a separate bowl or jug.

4 Add the wet ingredients to the dry ingredients and mix well.

5 Add one of the three flavour combinations listed below and stir well. (You could split the basic mixture in half and add one flavour combination to one half and another flavour combination to the other.)

6 Divide the mixture between the paper cases and bake for 25 minutes, until well risen and golden brown.

CHERRY TOMATO, CARROT AND THYME

100g carrot, peeled and grated
100g cherry tomatoes, diced
2 tbsp chopped fresh thyme

BUTTERNUT SQUASH AND SWEETCORN

100g butternut squash, peeled and grated
4 spring onions, finely sliced
50g tinned sweetcorn

COURGETTE AND HERBS

100g courgette, grated
1 tbsp chopped fresh thyme
1 tbsp snipped chives
1 tbsp chopped fresh basil

Mini PIZZA QUICHES

makes 6 quiches

sunflower oil, for greasing

3 tortilla wraps

4 cherry tomatoes, sliced

2 spring onions, finely sliced

50g chorizo slices, roughly chopped

50g Cheddar, grated

4 large eggs, beaten

FOR THE TOPPING

4 cherry tomatoes, sliced

1 courgette, thinly sliced with a vegetable peeler

handful of fresh basil leaves

If you love pizza, then give these a whirl! It's as easy as choosing your favourite pizza toppings and adding them to a simple mixture. Here I've included chorizo, a yummy Spanish sausage that's packed full of flavour. Once you've given this a go, why not jazz up your quiches with other exciting new ingredients!

1 Preheat the oven to 200°C/Fan 180°C/Gas 6 and grease a 6-hole muffin tin with oil.

2 Cut two 12cm-diameter circles from each tortilla wrap and use to line the tins.

3 Divide the tomatoes, spring onions, chorizo and cheese between the wraps, then top with the beaten egg. Lightly season then bake for 20–22 minutes, until the mixture is set in the centre.

4 Remove from the oven and top with slices of tomato, ribbons of courgette and fresh basil to serve.

Why not try this?
Turn these into veggie quiches by swapping the chorizo for slices of cooked vegetarian sausage.

Power-Packed ORZO PASTA

 125g orzo pasta

 75g broccoli, broken into tiny florets

 100g cooked chicken, diced

 150g tinned sweetcorn

 100g cherry tomatoes, quartered

 2 tbsp freshly chopped basil

FOR THE DRESSING

 4 tbsp light olive oil

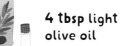 1 ½ tbsp rice wine vinegar

1 ½ tbsp soy sauce

 1 tbsp honey

Mamma mia! Everyone loves pasta! There are more than 600 types of pasta, so why not tick orzo off your list with this yummy recipe? Pasta is a good source of energy to fuel playtime, especially when combined with lots of healthy ingredients. What tasty medley will you make today?

1 Cook the pasta in lightly salted boiling water according to the packet instructions. Add the broccoli for the final 2 minutes of the cooking time. Drain and refresh in cold water.

2 Place the pasta, broccoli, chicken, sweetcorn, tomatoes and basil in a mixing bowl.

3 To make the dressing, combine all the ingredients in a small jug and mix well.

4 Just before serving, pour the tasty dressing over the salad and toss to coat.

Why not try this?
Stack the ingredients into a glass jar or Tupperware container to make a yummy picnic lunch. Keep the dressing separate until you're ready to eat.

CHICKEN and LETTUCE CUPS

1 large skinless chicken breast, sliced into strips

1 tbsp sunflower oil

6 round lettuce leaves

4 spring onions, finely sliced

1 carrot, peeled and sliced into thin strips

½ cucumber, sliced into thin strips

FOR THE MARINADE

1 clove garlic, peeled and crushed

2 tbsp soy sauce

2 tbsp sweet chilli sauce, plus extra to serve

1 tbsp brown sugar

juice of ½ lime

Wow friends and family with these bite-sized cups! Top the crunchy lettuce leaves with yummy chicken, cooked in my secret marinade (which is a sauce you make and add to the chicken before it is cooked). You'll be flavour of the month with this recipe!

1 To make the marinade, measure the garlic, soy sauce, sweet chilli sauce, sugar and lime juice into a bowl and mix together well. Add the chicken and leave to marinate for 30 minutes (or longer if possible, in which case, refrigerate).

2 Place the oil in a wok over a high heat. When the pan is very hot, add the chicken and marinade, and stir-fry for 3–4 minutes, until the chicken is cooked through and the marinade has reduced (which means thickened and intensified in flavour). Remove from the heat.

3 Arrange the lettuce leaves on a large serving plate. Place a little spring onion, carrot and cucumber inside each one. Divide the chicken mixture between them, then serve with some extra sweet chilli sauce.

Why not try this?
This marinade is also tasty when matched with strips of pork fillet or beef, and would make a great veggie dish with tofu.

veggie

egg free

makes 2 wraps

2 mini wraps

1 x portion of filling, see suggestions below

THAT'S A WRAP

Step aside soggy sarnies, there's a new lunchbox staple in town! My mini wraps are super fun to fill and eat, and once you've tried these four fab ideas, you can mix and match your own ingredients.

1 Warm the wraps in a dry frying pan over a medium heat, or for a few seconds in a microwave.

2 Divide the filling between the wraps – scattering the different ingredients evenly in a line along the centre of the wrap.

3 Roll up tightly and cut in half to serve.

RED ONION AND CHEESE

2 tbsp red onion marmalade
25g ready-grated mozzarella
25g Gruyère cheese, grated
handful of shredded lettuce

TUNA AND SWEETCORN

110g tuna in sunflower oil,
drained, mixed with 50g tinned
sweetcorn and 2 tbsp mayonnaise
2 spring onions, sliced
1 small carrot, peeled
and grated

PLUM AND CHICKEN

100g cooked diced chicken
handful of shredded lettuce
1/4 cucumber, cut into thin batons
2 spring onions, sliced
2 tsp mayonnaise
2 tsp plum sauce

CHICKEN, PESTO AND TOMATO

100g cooked chicken mixed
with 2 tbsp mayonnaise
and 1 tbsp pesto
handful of shredded lettuce
1/2 small avocado, diced
5 cherry tomatoes, quartered

makes 6-8 empanadas

EASY
Chicken and Tomato
EMPANADAS

 1½ tbsp olive oil

 ½ onion, peeled and roughly chopped

 1 clove garlic, peeled and crushed

 300g tinned chopped tomatoes

 1 tbsp sundried tomato paste or tomato purée

 2 tbsp freshly chopped basil or coriander

 75g cherry tomatoes, chopped

 75g ready-grated mozzarella

 100g cooked chicken, diced

 6-8 mini tortillas

I love to share food ideas from around the world. Have you heard of empanadas, which are popular in Latin America? They are delicious little parcels with a warm crust on the outside and a tasty filling on the inside. This is a simple twist on the empanada – best eaten with your hands for extra fun factor!

1 Place 1 tablespoon of the oil in a frying pan over a medium heat. Add the onion and garlic and fry for 3–4 minutes.

2 Stir in the tomatoes and sundried tomato paste or purée. Simmer for 5 minutes. Remove from the heat and leave to cool.

3 Mix the basil, cherry tomatoes, mozzarella, chicken and cooled tomato sauce in a bowl and season lightly.

4 Place a wrap on the surface and spoon some of the mixture over one half of it. Fold the empty side over the top, then set aside. Repeat with the other wraps and remaining mixture.

5 Heat the remaining oil in a large frying pan. Add the empanadas and fry for 2 minutes on each side, until lightly brown and the filling has melted. You can flip them using a spatula – place your hand on top of the empanada to prevent the filling spilling out, but take care to keep your hand away from the hot pan. You may need to cook them in batches.

egg free

veggie

makes 3 pizzas

freeze

PESTO PIZZAS

300g strong white bread flour

1 tsp dried yeast (from a sachet)

1 tsp salt

1 tbsp olive oil, plus extra for drizzling

FOR THE TOMATO SAUCE

1 tsp olive oil

1 onion, diced

1 clove garlic, crushed

250ml passata

1 tbsp tomato purée

FOR THE TOPPING

150g ready-grated mozzarella

6 cherry tomatoes, halved

6 tbsp pesto

small handful of fresh basil leaves

Turn into a budding baker as I teach you how to make pizza bases! Once you have them prepped, you can channel your inner Picasso with the toppings – make funny faces or colourful patterns.

1 To make the base, place the flour in a large bowl and stir in the yeast and salt. Make a well in the centre, pour in 200ml warm water and the olive oil, and stir together using a wooden spoon to make a soft, sticky dough.

2 Turn the dough out onto a floured work surface and knead for 5 minutes until smooth. Place the dough in a clean, lightly oiled bowl, cover with a tea towel and leave to rise for an hour in a warm place.

3 Meanwhile, to make the tomato sauce, place the oil and onion in a pan over a medium heat and sauté for 4 minutes. Add the garlic and sauté for 30 seconds. Add the passata and tomato purée, season lightly and cook for about 12 minutes, until thickened.

4 Preheat the oven to 240°C/Fan 220°C/Gas 9 and line a baking tray with non-stick paper.

5 Turn the dough out onto a floured work surface and knead again briefly. Divide into 3 balls and roll out each one using a rolling pin. Lift onto the baking tray.

6 Spread some tomato sauce over each pizza base, then add the toppings: sprinkle each one with cheese, top with the tomatoes and add 2 tablespoons of pesto to each pizza. Drizzle with a little olive oil and season with salt and pepper. Bake in the oven for 10 minutes.

7 Sprinkle over basil leaves to serve.

veggie

egg free

makes 4 portions

SUPER VEGGIE GNOCCHI

1 tbsp olive oil

2 banana shallots, peeled and finely sliced

1 red pepper, deseeded and diced

1 clove garlic, peeled and crushed

80g baby spinach

275g yellow and red cherry tomatoes, halved

400g gnocchi

150g crème fraîche

50g Parmesan, finely grated, plus extra to serve

3 tbsp fresh basil leaves

If you've never had gnocchi before, they're an Italian pasta-dumpling made from potato. I like to call them little fluffy pillows! Paired with my super-powered colourful veggie medley, this is a dinner winner!

1 Place the oil in a frying pan over a medium heat. Add the shallots and red pepper and fry for 3–4 minutes, until softened.

2 Stir in the garlic and fry for 10 seconds. Add the spinach and tomatoes and fry for a further 2 minutes.

3 Meanwhile, cook the gnocchi according to the packet instructions. Drain well.

4 Add the crème fraîche to the pan with the vegetables and bring to a simmer. Immediately remove from the heat, add the gnocchi, Parmesan and basil, season lightly with salt and pepper and toss together.

5 Serve in bowls with more Parmesan sprinkled over the top.

Why not try this?
Supercharge your gnocchi and pack in extra nutrition with cooked chicken or turkey.

1,2,3
FISH GOUJONS

makes 4 portions

200g skinless sole fillet, sliced into strips

50g plain flour

30g Panko breadcrumbs

20g Parmesan, finely grated

1 egg, beaten

2 tbsp sunflower oil, for frying

lemon wedges, for squeezing

FOR THE SOUR CREAM DIP (OPTIONAL)

150g sour cream

½ clove garlic, peeled and crushed

2 tsp freshly chopped chives

You'll love dipping the fish in the flour, egg and breadcrumbs to give it a special crunchy coating. It's as easy as 1, 2, 3! I've used Panko breadcrumbs, but you could also use Rice Krispies or crushed cornflakes to coat the fish. And why not try the same method but with chicken strips or salmon, too?

1 Season the fish with salt and pepper and coat in the flour.

2 Mix the breadcrumbs and Parmesan in a shallow bowl.

3 Dip each strip of sole into the beaten egg, then coat in the crumbs.

4 Heat the oil in a large frying pan over a medium heat. When hot, fry the goujons for about 5 minutes, turning halfway through the cooking time, until golden brown on both sides and cooked through.

5 Meanwhile, if making the dip, combine all the ingredients in a small bowl.

6 Serve the goujons with the dip, a lemon wedge for squeezing and some sweet potato fries (see page 64) and peas.

makes 4 portions

STICKY SALMON and Rice

Ingredients

1 tbsp ketchup

2 tbsp soy sauce

2 tsp sweet chilli sauce

150g salmon fillet, cut into large chunks

1 tbsp olive oil

a knob of butter

1 small onion, peeled and diced

½ red pepper, deseeded and diced

50g carrot, peeled and diced

50g courgette, diced

1 clove garlic, peeled and crushed

250g cooked basmati rice

2 tbsp frozen or tinned sweetcorn

small handful of fresh coriander leaves (optional)

Growing bodies needs many types of nutrients, and salmon is an excellent source of omega-3 fatty acids, which help brain growth and performance.
So eating salmon can actually make you smarter! Here's a clever Asian-inspired idea that is packed with flavour.

1 Preheat the oven to 200°C/Fan 180°C/Gas 6. Line a baking sheet with foil.

2 Mix the ketchup, half the soy sauce and half the sweet chilli sauce together in a bowl. Add the salmon and coat in the mixture.

3 Spoon onto the baking sheet and cook in the oven for 10 minutes, until just cooked through.

4 Meanwhile, place the oil and butter in a frying pan over a medium heat. Add the onion, pepper and carrot and fry for a few minutes. Add the courgette and garlic and fry for a further 2 minutes.

5 Stir in the rice and sweetcorn and toss over the heat.

6 Season with the remaining soy and sweet chilli sauces. Divide the rice between four plates and top with the salmon pieces and coriander, if using.

Why not try this?
Go veggie by swapping the salmon for tofu. Simply dust in flour, marinate in the sauce and add to the pan with the courgette and garlic.

Meat and Fish

Meat and fish provide us with an all-important source of protein in our diets which we need to grow and maintain our muscles and body tissues.

TRY THIS!

Ship ahoy! Oily fish such as salmon, mackerel and sardines are packed with essential omega-3 fatty acids which give our brains a boost to help make us smarter! So, try to have two portions of oily fish per week.

IRON

If you don't eat enough iron from certain foods you can start to feel tired and weak. Here are some good sources for you to explore!

Did you know?

People who follow a vegetarian diet don't eat meat or animal products. Instead, they eat eggs, nuts and seeds, pulses, beans, fruits and veggies. In fact, everyone should enjoy these nutritious foods for a well-balanced diet!

Chicken

Beef

Egg yolks

Cereals

Dried fruits

Pulses

Excellent Eggs

Boiled, poached, fried or scrambled, eggs are a nutritious way to fuel your day!

THE SPINNING TRICK

You can check whether an egg is cooked or raw by spinning it on its side. A raw egg will spin slowly and shakily, but a boiled egg will spin steadily and fast!

PERFECT BOILED EGGS EVERY TIME!

★ Fill a medium sized saucepan with water and bring to a rolling boil.

★ Make sure your eggs aren't fridge cold. Having the eggs at room temperature will stop them from cracking.

★ Slowly lower the eggs into the water using a spoon. Make sure a grown-up is on hand to help!

★ Allow 4–5 minutes for runny eggs to serve with dippy soldiers.

★ Allow 6–7 minutes for soft-boiled eggs.

Tip: If serving soft boiled eggs in a salad, plunge them into a bowl of cold water as soon as the timer goes off – this will stop them cooking and cool the shells quickly for peeling.

GOOD EGG, BAD EGG?

If you want to find out whether an egg is still fresh, just place it in a bowl of water. If the egg sinks to the bottom it is fine to eat, but if it floats to the top it's old and worth giving a miss!

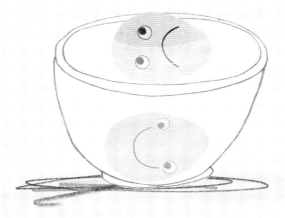

HOW TO PEEL AN EGG

Peeling hard-boiled eggs can be tricky! Here are some simple tips.

★ Crack the egg all over by tapping it on your counter.

★ Roll the egg gently between your hands to loosen the shell.

★ Peel the egg starting at the large end. Dip the egg in a bowl of water to help remove the shell.

Sunshine PAELLA

 1 tbsp olive oil

 1 large onion, peeled and roughly chopped

 1 small red pepper, deseeded and diced

 1 large clove garlic, peeled and crushed

 175g paella or risotto rice

 ½ tsp ground turmeric

 1 tsp tomato purée

 600ml chicken stock

 2 cooked sausages, sliced

 75g cooked chicken, cut into chunks

 150g cooked small prawns

 50g frozen peas

 squeeze lemon juice

 1 tbsp freshly chopped parsley or coriander (optional)

Paella is a famous Spanish rice dish, and I love its bright yellow sunshine colour! I call this my one-pot 'cheat's' paella, as it's so easy to make. The best thing about this traditional dish is that anything goes. You can add whatever meat, fish or veggies you like, so it's time to roll up those sleeves and get stirring!

1 Place the oil in a large, shallow frying pan over a medium heat. Add the onion and pepper and fry for 2 minutes. Stir in the garlic and fry for 10 seconds.

2 Add the rice, turmeric and tomato purée and stir.

3 Pour in the chicken stock and bring to the boil. Reduce the heat to a simmer, cover with a lid and leave to cook for about 20 minutes, until the rice is nearly cooked.

4 Stir in the sausages, chicken, prawns and peas, cover again and cook for a final 5 minutes.

5 Season with salt and pepper, and add the lemon juice and parsley or coriander, if using, just before serving.

Why not try this?

Mussels are a traditional ingredient in seafood paella. Wash them well and ensure the shells are closed before cooking. When the rice is almost ready, add the mussels, pushing them down into the rice. Continue to cook until the mussels have opened. Never eat a mussel that hasn't opened during cooking.

POPCORN CHICKEN
and Sweet Potato Fries

 25g Rice Krispies

 25g salted popcorn

 15g Parmesan,
finely grated

 2 skinless
chicken breasts,
cut into chunks

 50g plain flour

 2 eggs, beaten

**FOR THE SWEET
POTATO FRIES**

 1 large sweet
potato, peeled and
cut into fries about
4mm wide

 ½ tbsp cornflour

 1 tbsp mild olive oil

I call this my movie night recipe – check out the main ingredient in this crunchy chicken coating! It is a whole new way to serve chicken and chips, packing in one of your 5-a-day. Sweet potato fries make the best chips, but spread them out on the tray to ensure they go nice and crispy!

1 Preheat the oven to 220°C/Fan 200°C/Gas 7. Line two baking trays with non-stick paper.

2 Arrange the sweet potato fries in a single layer on one of the trays. Sprinkle over the cornflour and then the olive oil, rubbing in any visible cornflour. Season with a little salt and pepper and bake for 20–25 minutes, turning halfway through, until crispy.

3 Meanwhile, measure the Rice Krispies, popcorn and a good pinch of salt into a polythene bag. Bash the bag with a rolling pin to crush into fine crumbs. Add the Parmesan and shake to mix.

4 Coat the chicken in seasoned flour, then dip into the beaten egg. Cover each piece of chicken in the crumbs, then place on the second baking sheet. Bake in the oven for 10 minutes, until lightly golden and cooked through.

5 Serve the popcorn chicken with the fries.

Why not try this?
Try coating chunks of halloumi in the popcorn mix. Fry over a medium heat in a little oil, to make a veggie version of this dish.

makes 10–12 burgers

Teddy Bear BURGERS

1 tsp sunflower oil

10–12 small brioche buns (or make your own mini rolls using the bread dough on page 82)

10–12 soft lettuce leaves

FOR THE BURGER MIX

1 onion, peeled and roughly chopped

1 apple, peeled, cored and grated

1 small clove garlic, peeled and crushed

500g minced beef

100g fine breadcrumbs

75g Parmesan, finely grated

1 tbsp chopped fresh thyme

1 tsp Worcestershire sauce

My homemade burgers are bound to be a hit with the whole family. My surprise ingredient? A little grated apple to add a spot of natural sweetness. Don't forget to make enough for mummy and daddy bear!

1 Measure the onion, apple and garlic into a food processor and blend until finely chopped, or finely dice by hand. Tip into a bowl with the remaining burger ingredients, lightly season and mix together well. Shape into 10–12 burgers.

2 Place the oil in a large frying pan over a medium-high heat. Add the burgers and fry for 3–4 minutes on each side, until brown and cooked through. Alternatively, cook the burgers under a preheated grill for about 5 minutes on each side.

3 Meanwhile, slice the buns in half and place a lettuce leaf on each base. Top with a burger and finish with the top half of the bun.

Why not try this?

Turn your burgers into teddy bears! Stamp out a small oval shape from a slice of Cheddar. Stick a small piece of black olive onto the cheese to make a nose and two strips for the mouth. Place two slices of olive on the bun for the eyes. Slice a frankfurter to make ears and stamp out a small oval of Cheddar to place in the middle of each ear. Attach them using cocktail sticks on either side of the face.

5-A-Day Fruit and Veg

Some of the most bright, colourful and exciting food is also some of the healthiest! Fruits and vegetables come in all shapes and sizes – from bright yellow bananas to spiky pineapples, purple curly kale, flower-like artichokes and... fun looking (and sounding) dragon fruit!

Did you know?

The tangy fuzzy kiwi fruit contains nearly twice as much Vitamin C as an orange so why not add to your fruit salad or yoghurt, or blend to make ice lollies!

PEEL BANANAS LIKE A MONKEY

While most of us peel bananas from the stem down, it often bruises them and turns the top to mush. We should copy monkeys and turn our bananas upside down and pinch the base. The banana then splits easily and you can peel it back ready to eat!

HOW TO TURN GRAPES INTO RAISINS!

Did you know that drying grapes in the sun turns them into raisins? You can do this in the kitchen too!

★ Preheat the oven to a low heat about 110°C/Fan 90°C/Gas ¼.

★ Arrange red grapes on a baking sheet lined with baking paper and bake in the oven for about 4 hours. Et voilà! One supercharged snack at the ready.

LET'S COUNT OUR 5-A-DAY!

We should all be eating at least FIVE portions of different fruits and vegetables every day – grown-ups included!

As a guide, 1 portion = the amount you can fit in the palm of your hand.

Did you know?
Some foods we think of as vegetables are actually fruit as they contain seeds – tomatoes, peppers and aubergine are all fruit!

GROW IT!

All you need is cress seeds, cotton wool and a cute container.

1 Soak cotton wool in a shallow container and sprinkle seeds on top.

2 Spray regularly with water to make sure the cotton wool stays moist.

3 Your cress will start to shoot up in 2 to 3 days!

Tip: Try growing your cress in eggshells filled with cotton wool!

1 tbsp olive oil

1 small onion, peeled and finely chopped

1 small leek, trimmed and thinly sliced

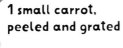

½ stick celery, diced

½ small red pepper, deseeded and diced

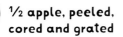

1 small carrot, peeled and grated

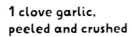

50g mushrooms, diced

½ apple, peeled, cored and grated

1 clove garlic, peeled and crushed

1 x 400g tin chopped tomatoes

450g minced beef

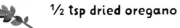

4 tbsp tomato purée

2 tbsp ketchup

250ml beef stock

½ tsp dried oregano

1 tbsp grated Parmesan

small handful of fresh basil leaves

makes 6 portions   **freeze**   **gluten free**   **egg free**

VROOM VROOM
VEGGIE-PACKED BOLOGNESE

After a busy day, this is the perfect way to recharge your batteries. Plus, it's packed with lots of good-for-you veggies. Get. Set. Go!

1 Place the oil in a large frying pan over a medium heat. Add the vegetables and apple and fry for 10 minutes until soft. Stir in the garlic and fry for 10 seconds.

2 Transfer to a blender, add the chopped tomatoes and whizz until smooth. Set aside.

3 Add the mince to the frying pan and place over a medium-high heat. Fry for 4 minutes, breaking the mince up with a wooden spoon, until browned (you may need to do this in batches).

4 Place the tomato and vegetable sauce in the pan with the mince, then add the tomato purée, ketchup, stock and oregano. Bring to a simmer and cook for 40–45 minutes, until the sauce is thick. Season to taste with salt and pepper.

5 Serve with spaghetti and a sprinkling of Parmesan and fresh basil leaves.

FRUITY Chicken Korma

 1 tbsp mild olive oil or sunflower oil

 2 skinless chicken breasts, cut into chunks

 1 onion, peeled and roughly chopped

 1 carrot, peeled and diced

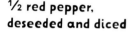 ½ red pepper, deseeded and diced

 1 apple, peeled, cored and diced

 ½ tsp grated fresh root ginger

 1½ tbsp korma curry paste

 200ml full-fat coconut milk

 200ml chicken stock

 1 tbsp mango chutney

 1 tsp soy sauce

 50g frozen peas

 small handful of fresh coriander leaves (optional)

It's time for a curry night! Indian food is packed with colour and flavour, and I've designed this mild, fruity curry especially for kids. Watch out, though, because grown-ups will love it, too!

1 Place the oil in a deep frying pan over a high heat. Season the chicken and fry quickly until browned and sealed. Remove from the pan and set aside.

2 Reduce the heat, add the onion, carrot, pepper and apple to the pan and fry for 5 minutes, stirring occasionally. Stir in the ginger and curry paste and fry for 30 seconds.

3 Pour in the coconut milk and bring up to the boil. Reduce the heat and simmer for 5 minutes.

4 Season lightly, stir the browned chicken, mango chutney, soy sauce and peas into the curry and simmer for a final 5 minutes, until the chicken is cooked through.

5 Sprinkle with the coriander, if using, and serve with rice and poppadums.

Why not try this?
Make your own curry paste – combine 1 tbsp cumin seeds, 50g cashews, 4 tbsp tomato purée, 1 small bunch fresh coriander, 2 peeled cloves garlic, 15g desiccated coconut, 1 tbsp garam masala and 3 tsp finely grated fresh ginger in a small food processor and whizz to a paste. Store in a sterilised jar in the fridge or freeze in portions.

125g medium egg noodles

1 tbsp sunflower oil

200g sirloin steak, sliced into strips

1 onion, peeled and finely sliced

1 red pepper, deseeded and finely sliced

100g baby corn, sliced lengthways

150g button mushrooms, sliced

100g sugar snap peas, sliced lengthways

225g Chinese leaves, thinly sliced

2 cloves garlic, peeled and crushed

1 tsp honey

2 tbsp oyster sauce

1 tbsp hoisin sauce

1 tbsp soy sauce

Sizzlin' STIR-FRY

Woks at the ready! It's time to wow your family with my fast, fresh stir-fry. This is a method of cooking that came from China. Fancy having a go? Make sure you have all your ingredients cut up and ready before you start. Chop, chop!

1 Cook the noodles according to the packet instructions. Drain and rinse under cold water, then set aside.

2 Place the oil in a large frying pan or wok over a high heat. Season the steak with salt and pepper, add to the pan and stir-fry for 1–2 minutes, until brown and just cooked. Remove from the pan with a slotted spoon and set aside.

3 Add the onion, pepper, baby corn, mushrooms, sugar snap peas and Chinese leaves to the pan and stir-fry for 1–2 minutes. Add the garlic and fry for 10 seconds.

4 Return the beef to the pan and add the noodles, honey and oyster, hoisin and soy sauces. Toss everything together over the heat, then serve at once.

Why not try this?

Make this veggie by using Quorn fillet instead of beef. There's no need to fry the slices first – just add with the veg.

50g white bread, torn into small pieces

6 tbsp milk

350g lean beef mince

50g Parmesan, grated

1 egg yolk

2 tbsp chopped fresh thyme

1 tbsp olive oil

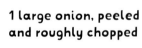

1 large onion, peeled and roughly chopped

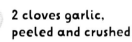

2 cloves garlic, peeled and crushed

2 x 400g tins chopped tomatoes

2 tbsp tomato purée

pinch of sugar

3 tbsp freshly chopped basil

200g fusilli pasta

50g **Cheddar**, grated

125g ready-grated mozzarella

MIGHTY Meatball Pasta Bake

Serve up this meaty dish and there'll be clean plates all round! Beef is a great source of iron, which is what makes this recipe so MIGHTY. Aprons on – this pasta bake means business!

1 Place the bread and milk in a large bowl and leave to soak for 5 minutes.

2 Mash the bread and milk together, then add the beef, Parmesan, egg yolk and 1 tablespoon of the thyme and season lightly. Mix well, then shape into 30 little balls.

3 Place half the oil in a large frying pan over a medium heat. Add the meatballs and fry for 8 minutes, until browned. Remove from the pan and set aside.

4 Add the remaining oil and the onion to the pan and fry for 5 minutes, until nearly soft. Add the garlic and fry for 10 seconds. Stir in the tomatoes, purée, remaining thyme and the sugar. Cover and simmer for 15 minutes.

5 Return the meatballs to the pan and cook for another 10 minutes. Season and stir in the basil.

6 Meanwhile, cook the pasta according to the packet instructions. Drain the pasta and stir it into the sauce. Spoon everything into an oven dish and sprinkle with the cheeses.

7 Preheat the grill to high.

8 Place the dish under the grill and cook for 10 minutes, or until the cheeses have melted.

Snacks and treats

egg free

gluten free

veggie

serves 4

LEO LION VEGGIE DIP

You'll have a 'roaring' time making this fun dip with colourful veggies! Hummus is packed with protein and this jungle showstopper makes the perfect snack or 'mane' event at the party table. Let's see how many colourful veggies you can find to make Leo shine.

1 Place the chickpeas, garlic and olive oil in a food processor and whizz until blended, or blitz with a hand blender. Add the sour cream and lemon juice and blend again until smooth.

2 Spoon into a small serving bowl and place the bowl on a large plate.

3 Arrange the carrots and peppers around the bowl to serve.

1 x 400g tin chickpeas, drained and rinsed

1 clove garlic, peeled and crushed

3 tbsp olive oil

150g sour cream

juice of ½ lemon

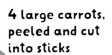
4 large carrots, peeled and cut into sticks

½ yellow pepper, deseeded and sliced

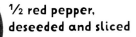
½ red pepper, deseeded and sliced

Why not try this?
Let's make a lion's face! Cut or stamp out bread for the ears, eyes and cheeks. Pop the bread eyes on top of the dip and add slices of grapes for the eyeballs. Add the cheeks and make a nose with half a grape. The tongue could be a small slice of red pepper. To finish, arrange chives either side for the whiskers.

veggie

dairy free

freeze

serves 4

SNAIL DOUGH BALLS

We've all made snails and animal shapes with playdough, but how about using real bread dough? If you're a mini baker, my yummy snail 'tear and share' is a must. Anyone slow to the table will miss out, as these freshly baked dough balls are a winner.

300g strong white bread flour

7g dried yeast (from a sachet)

1 tsp salt

1 tbsp olive oil, plus extra for greasing

200ml warm water

1 egg, beaten

FOR THE GARLIC BUTTER DIP (OPTIONAL)

50g soft butter

1 clove garlic, peeled and crushed

Why not try this?
Use whole olives as antennae (little ones will need these halved before eating) and slices of olive to create a snail face!

1 Measure the flour, yeast and salt into a bowl. Add the oil and water and mix to a soft dough.

2 Turn out onto a lightly floured work surface and knead the dough until smooth. Place in a clean, lightly oiled bowl, cover with clingfilm or a tea towel and leave to rise for 2 hours, or until doubled in size.

3 Preheat the oven to 220°C/Fan 200°C/Gas 7 and line a baking tray with non-stick paper.

4 Knock the dough back, then divide into about 30 balls.

5 Arrange the balls on the baking tray in the shape of a snail. Cover with clingfilm and leave to prove for 30 minutes.

6 Brush the dough with the beaten egg and bake for 25–30 minutes, or until well risen and lightly golden.

7 Meanwhile, if making the dip, mix the butter, garlic and a pinch of salt in a small bowl.

8 Remove the bread from the oven and serve warm with the garlic butter.

TOMATO AND SWEETCORN FRITTER Stack

veggie

makes 8 fritters

120g tinned sweetcorn

8 cherry tomatoes, roughly chopped

½ clove garlic, peeled and roughly chopped

1 tbsp sweet chilli sauce

100g plain flour

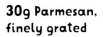
½ tsp baking powder

30g Parmesan, finely grated

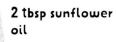
1 egg, beaten

2 tbsp sunflower oil

We all love sweetcorn! It's bright, juicy and sweet, and a fantastic food to fuel a growing body. Did you know that it comes fresh, frozen and tinned? That means you'll always have some ready to make these stackable treats. My fritters are the perfect dippers – try them with hummus, sour cream or sweet chilli sauce. Flip, stack, then dip!

1 Place the sweetcorn in a food processor or hand blender and whizz until roughly chopped.

2 Scoop into a bowl and add all the remaining ingredients except the oil. Lightly season and mix well.

3 Place the oil in a frying pan over a medium heat. Spoon large tablespoonfuls of the sweetcorn mixture into the pan. Spread out slightly with the back of a spoon and fry for 3–4 minutes. Turn the fritters and fry for a few minutes on the other side, until lightly browned and cooked through.

Why not try this?
Turn this into a breakfast winner by topping the fritters with a fried egg. You'll love dunking the fritters into the yummy yolk.

egg
free

freeze

veggie

makes 12
pieces

CHOCOLATE
Fridge Cake

 75g plain chocolate, broken into pieces

 125g milk chocolate, broken into pieces

 50g unsalted butter

 2 tbsp golden syrup

 100g double cream

 175g Digestive biscuits, broken into small pieces

 20g mini marshmallows

 75g dried apricots, chopped

 50g raisins

 50g pecans, finely chopped

 25g Rice Krispies

Explorers need plenty of fuel for their adventures, and this nutty snack is an essential for any quest! Whether you're building forts and castles, a camp, or escaping into the great outdoors, don't leave without your explorer snack!

1 Line a 20cm square shallow tin with clingfilm, leaving enough to hang over the sides.

2 Place the plain and milk chocolate, the butter, golden syrup and cream in a fairly large, heatproof bowl over a pan of simmering water. Make sure the bottom of the bowl doesn't touch the water. Allow to melt slowly, stirring occasionally.

3 Remove from the heat and add the remaining ingredients to the bowl, stirring so that everything is coated in the chocolate mixture.

4 Spoon into the prepared tin and level the surface by pressing down with a potato masher or the back of a spoon.

5 Leave to cool in the tin, then transfer to the fridge and leave to set for 1–2 hours.

6 To serve, carefully lift out of the tin, then peel off the clingfilm and cut into triangles.

Why not try this?
Swap the Rice Krispies for cornflakes for an extra crispy, cool crunch.

BEAR BRUNCH MUFFINS

 150g self-raising flour

 ½ tsp baking powder

 50g caster sugar

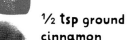 ½ tsp ground cinnamon

 ½ tsp ground ginger

 125ml sunflower oil

75ml maple syrup

 2 medium eggs, lightly beaten

 ½ tsp vanilla extract

 1 apple, peeled, cored and grated

75g carrots, peeled and grated

 50g raisins

No teddy bear picnic is complete without these fun treats. Batch cook them and your friends and family will be sure of a big surprise! Not only do they taste bear-licious, they also include secret ingredients – carrot and apple – to help towards your 5-a-day.

1 Preheat the oven to 180°C/Fan 160°C/Gas 4 and line a 12-hole muffin tin with paper cases.

2 Measure the flour, baking powder, sugar, cinnamon and ginger into a large mixing bowl.

3 Combine the oil, maple syrup, eggs and vanilla in a separate large bowl and beat lightly with a whisk until blended.

4 Add the grated apple, carrots and raisins to the liquid mixture, then fold in the dry ingredients until just combined. Be careful not to over mix.

5 Fill the muffin cases until two thirds full and bake in the oven for 20–25 minutes.

6 Remove from the oven and leave to cool in the tin for 5 minutes, then transfer to a wire rack to cool completely.

Why not try this?
Make your muffins into mini bears – slice an apricot in half for ears, place a whole apricot with a raisin on top for a nose, then finish with some edible eyes.

egg free

freeze

veggie

makes 16 cookies

CHAMPION Choc Chip COOKIES

 100g soft butter

 75g light brown sugar

1 tbsp golden syrup

 170g self-raising flour

pinch of salt

 ½ tsp vanilla extract

   50g plain chocolate chips

Hands up if you're a little cookie monster? If so, my soft and chewy recipe certainly takes the biscuit. Squish your favourite ice cream in between two cookies for an ice-cool treat.

1 Preheat the oven to 200°C/Fan 180°C/Gas 6 and line 2 baking sheets with non-stick paper.

2 Measure the butter and sugar into a bowl and beat with an electric whisk until the mixture has lightened in colour.

3 Add the golden syrup, flour, salt, vanilla and chocolate chips and bring the mixture together using your hands.

4 Knead lightly then shape into 16 balls. Place them on the baking sheets and flatten slightly with the back of a spoon. Bake for about 10 minutes, until golden.

5 Remove from the oven and leave to cool slightly on the trays before transferring to a wire rack to cool completely.

Why not try this?
Make a chocolate and orange cookie instead by swapping the self-raising flour with 120g self-raising flour and 25g cocoa powder, and adding 1 tsp of orange extract instead of the vanilla.

Sweet Things

We all enjoy a sweet-tasting treat every now and then, and sugar can also be found naturally in lots of foods like fruit, vegetables, milk and honey.

SUGAR

Sugar comes from sugar cane or sugar beet plants. The sugar juice is extracted and that's when the magic happens! It can be ground up to make finer sugars like caster sugar for baking or powdered to make icing sugar – perfect to sprinkle over cakes!

CHOCOLATE

Chocolate is made by combining sugar and milk with cocoa, which comes from the beans of the cacao plant.

The ancient Aztecs in Central America used to pay with cacao beans instead of money!

MELT IT!

Lots of recipes call for melted chocolate, so here's how:

1 Break chocolate into chunks.

2 Put into a heatproof bowl over a pan of simmering water and stir occasionally until melted. Just don't let the water touch the base of the bowl. Chocolate is very delicate and can become lumpy and grainy if overheated.

3 You can also put chocolate chunks in a suitable bowl and heat in a microwave in 20 second bursts, stirring in between until melted.

Did you know?

Chocolate melts at body temperature which is why it melts on your tongue...if you let it stay there long enough that is!

HONEY FROM THE BEES!

Busy bees make delicious golden honey, which is as sweet as sugar and perfect for spreading on toast or drizzling over pancakes.

Did you know?

You can make sugar-free pancakes using overripe bananas instead of sugar. Bananas get brown spots and become extra sweet when they've been in the fruit bowl too long. You can add these overripe bananas to pancake mixes, banana bread or blend to make ice cream (the browner the banana the better!).

Bees produce honey as food stores for the hive during winter but luckily for us, these efficient little workers produce 2–3 times more honey than they need, so we get to enjoy the tasty treat, too!

BEE-EAUTIFUL!

Have you seen busy bees buzzing around the garden? They're actually busy making honey!

1 Bees collect sugary nectar from flowers. One of the reasons why flowers are so bright and colourful is to help bees find the nectar.

2 The nectar is taken back to the hive and stored in honeycomb.

3 Bees fan the honeycomb so that the nectar thickens into honey.

4 Bees seal the honey inside the honeycomb with beeswax, storing all the sweetness in tiny hexagons!

veggie

freeze

makes 15
cookies

65g soft butter

50g soft dark
brown sugar

4 tbsp
golden syrup

1 egg yolk

175g plain flour

1 tsp ground ginger

½ tsp bicarbonate
of soda

generous pinch
of salt

GINGERSNAP COOKIES

Spiced biscuits are an all-year-round favourite, and you can use any cutter shapes you like. Animals are fun to decorate but any will work. Mild spices, like the ginger in this recipe, are a great way to introduce more flavour to foods. Let's swap bland and boring for tasty and tantalising!

1 Measure the butter and sugar into a large bowl and beat with an electric whisk until pale.

2 Add the golden syrup, egg yolk, flour, ginger, bicarbonate of soda and salt and beat again until a dough forms.

3 Mould the dough into a large ball with your hands, wrap in clingfilm and chill for at least 30 minutes.

4 Preheat the oven to 180°C/Fan 160°C/Gas 4 and line two baking sheets with non-stick paper.

5 Place the dough on a floured work surface and, starting in the centre of the dough and rolling evenly outwards, roll the dough to a thickness of about 3mm. Cut into shapes using cookie cutters. Re-roll the trimmings until all the dough is used up.

6 Place the cookies on the baking sheets and bake for about 10 minutes, until golden.

7 Remove from the oven and leave to cool slightly on the tray before transferring to a wire rack to cool completely.

makes
16 balls

125g smooth
peanut butter

50g salted butter

50g Rice Krispies

75g icing sugar

Peanut Butter POPS

Look out for the snap, crackle and pop ingredient in this recipe! Add protein-packed peanut butter and you have a scrummy snack in no time. Try dipping them in natural yoghurt or, as an extra special treat, why not dunk them in melted chocolate?

1 Place the peanut butter and butter in a small saucepan over a low heat. Stir together until melted.

2 Meanwhile, combine the Rice Krispies and icing sugar in a large bowl.

3 Pour the peanut butter mixture into the bowl with the Rice Krispies and stir with a wooden spoon until combined.

4 Using your hands, roll the mixture into 16 small balls and place on a plate in the fridge for about 40 minutes to firm up.

Why not try this?

Here's a tip if you're going to dip these pops in chocolate: leave them to set in an empty ice cube tray – this will help the chocolate harden evenly.

ANIMAL Cupcakes

These fun bakes are perfect for party animals! Once your cakes are baked and cooled, why not create pups, pandas and cheeky monkeys? Or you can decorate them with your own favourite animals.

FOR THE CAKES

2 large eggs

100g soft butter

100g caster sugar

150g self-raising flour

1 tsp baking powder

2 tbsp milk

1 tsp vanilla extract

FOR THE ICING

200g soft butter

1 tbsp milk

300g icing sugar

1 Preheat the oven to 180°C/Fan 160°C/Gas 4 and line a 12-hole muffin tin with paper cases.

2 Measure all the cake ingredients into a large bowl and beat together using an electric whisk until light and fluffy.

3 Spoon the mixture into the paper cases and bake for 20–25 minutes, until golden.

4 Remove from the oven and transfer to a wire rack to cool.

5 Meanwhile, to make the icing, place the butter, milk and icing sugar in a large bowl. Beat together using an electric whisk until fluffy and pale.

6 Once the cupcakes are cool, spread or pipe the icing on top and serve.

PUPPY DOGS

Add 25g cocoa powder to the icing and pipe it onto the cakes. Cut ear shapes out of brown fondant and add edible eyes, a jellybean nose and a piece of pink lace for a tongue.

PANDAS

Dip the iced cupcakes in desiccated coconut (you will need about 75g for all 12 cakes). Cut noses, mouths and oval shapes from black fondant and place edible eyes on top. Add mini Oreos for ears.

MONKEYS

Turn the icing brown with 25g cocoa powder and ice the cakes, then dip them in chocolate sprinkles. Use half a mini Jaffa Cake for each ear, and a whole one for the face, drawing on nostrils and a mouth with black fondant. Lastly, add edible eyes.

98 snacks and treats

CHOCOLATE FOOTBALL CUPCAKES

FOR THE CAKES

125g soft butter

125g caster sugar

2 eggs

100g self-raising flour

1 tsp baking powder

25g cocoa powder

2 tbsp milk

FOR THE ICING

100g soft butter

150g icing sugar

1 tsp vanilla extract

green food colouring

FOR THE DECORATION

white fondant

black fondant

It's time to set your ball skills aside and swot up on those decorating skills. The crowd will go wild for these yummy treats.

1 Follow the cupcake baking instructions from page 98, adding 25g cocoa powder to the mix.

2 Meanwhile, make the icing by measuring the butter, icing sugar and vanilla extract into a bowl. Beat together using an electric whisk until fluffy and pale. Mix in a little green food colouring.

3 Once the cupcakes are cool, spread or pipe the butter icing on top.

4 To turn the cupcakes into footballs, roll 10 little balls from white fondant and 6 little balls from black fondant. Arrange 5 white balls around 1 black ball, then place the remaining white balls on the ends of the white balls to make a star shape. Place the remaining black balls in the gaps between and squash them together. Cover the icing with clingfilm and roll out lightly to flatten the pattern together. Remove the clingfilm and stamp out a neat circle using a round cutter. Repeat to make another 11 toppers. Place on top of the cupcakes.

Why not try this?
Why not pick your favourite ball at home and try to recreate this on top of your cupcake?

100 snacks and treats

OAT and RAISIN POWER COOKIES

85g soft butter

50g soft light brown sugar

1 tbsp golden syrup

1 tsp vanilla extract

75g self-raising flour

½ tsp bicarbonate of soda

½ tsp salt

75g porridge oats

30g raisins

Fill the biscuit tin (and empty it just as quickly) with these easy oat and raisin cookies. Oats are awesome, as they provide you with hours of energy for your busy body and brain. Simply pair with a cold glass of milk for dunking.

1 Preheat the oven to 180°C/Fan 160°C/Gas 4 and line two large baking sheets with non-stick paper.

2 Measure the butter, sugar and syrup into a large mixing bowl and beat with an electric whisk until light and fluffy.

3 Stir in the remaining ingredients and beat again until the mixture comes together.

4 Divide into 12 balls and place them on the baking sheets, leaving space between each one to allow for spreading. Press down slightly to flatten and bake for 12 minutes, until lightly golden.

5 Remove from the oven and leave to cool slightly on the sheets before transferring to a wire rack to cool completely.

Why not try this?

Why not swap out raisins for dried cranberries for a festive treat? Or cut up those chocolate Mini Eggs from the Easter Bunny and add them to the mix!

Tutti Frutti
ICE LOLLIES

YOU WILL NEED

lolly mould

ice lolly sticks

Ice, ice, baby! It's time to get mixing your favourite fruity flavours to create a bright vitamin-packed treat! Whipping up a batch of homemade lollies is the perfect after-school energy boost. Don't forget to experiment with different flavours, such as beetroot and kiwi. Three different flavours, one simple method.

1 Combine all the ingredients in a blender and whizz until smooth.

2 Pour into an ice lolly mould, insert the sticks and place in the freezer for 4 hours, or until frozen.

PEACH, MANGO BANANA AND ORANGE

1 ripe peach, peeled and de-stoned
½ small mango, peeled and de-stoned
½ small ripe banana, peeled
juice of 1 orange

STRAWBERRY, APPLE AND BANANA

175g strawberries
½ ripe banana, peeled
100ml apple juice

BEETROOT, PEAR AND BLUEBERRY

50g cooked beetroot
100g blueberries
1 small ripe pear, peeled and cored
½ small ripe banana, peeled
100ml apple juice

veggie

egg free

makes 12 monsters

Krispie MONSTERS

100g butter

200g golden syrup

100g white chocolate, broken into pieces

225g Rice Krispies

FOR THE DECORATION

100g white chocolate, melted

A few drops of 3 different food colouring

White fondant

24 chocolate chips

Fancy making my boggle-eyed monster bars? They are always a Halloween hit, but you can make them any time of the year. Crank up your cauldron (AKA the hob) and have some food fun!

1 Line a 20cm square tin with non-stick paper.

2 Measure the butter and golden syrup into a saucepan, and stir over a medium heat until melted.

3 Remove from the heat and add the white chocolate. Stir until melted.

4 Add the Rice Krispies and a pinch of salt to the pan, and stir well until completely covered.

5 Spoon into the tin, spreading out and levelling the surface with the back of a spoon. Place in the fridge and chill for 4 hours or until firm.

6 Lift out of the tin and cut into 12 bars.

7 Divide the melted white chocolate into 3 small bowls and add a different food colouring to each bowl. Dip the bars halfway into the coloured chocolate and leave to set on non-stick paper.

8 Roll the white fondant into 24 little balls and push a chocolate chip into the centre of each one. Stick the eyes on to make monster faces.

Watermelon and Kiwi Lollies

275g watermelon, peeled and deseeded

2 kiwis, peeled

makes 6 lollies

1 Place the watermelon in a jug and blend until smooth using a stick blender.

2 Pour the purée into 6 ice lolly moulds, insert lolly sticks and freeze for 4 hours.

3 Meanwhile, blend the kiwis until smooth using a stick blender.

4 Remove the lollies from the freezer and pour the kiwi purée on top of the watermelon. Freeze again for 2–3 hours, or until completely frozen.

Pineapple and Strawberry Lollies

100ml pineapple juice

100g strawberries, sliced

makes 6 lollies

1 Pour the pineapple juice into the base of 6 ice lolly moulds and freeze for 1 hour.

2 Insert the sticks into the semi-frozen juice and place two slices of strawberries in each mould.

3 Place the remaining strawberries in a jug and blend until smooth using a stick blender. Pour the purée on top of the strawberry slices and freeze for 2 hours, or until completely frozen.

Index

About
Annabel Karmel

With expertise spanning 30 years, London-born mother of three Annabel Karmel reigns as the UK's no. 1 children's cookery author, bestselling international author, and a world-leading expert on devising delicious, nutritious meals for babies, children and families.

Since launching her revolutionary cookbook for babies – *The Complete Baby and Toddler Meal Planner* in 1991 – a feeding 'bible', which has become the second bestselling non-fiction hardback of all time, Annabel has cooked up 47 cookbooks and raised millions of families on her recipes.

Annabel's vision has always been to ensure every child gets the nutrients they need for their development and long-term health, and her unique, healthy recipe combinations and advice have made her a true pioneer in her field.

A powerhouse among parents, Annabel's trusty cookbooks can be found in family kitchens all over the world. She also connects with 1.5 million families on a weekly basis via her website and social media community. And most parents will have Annabel's #1 rated recipe app safely installed on their smart phones for on-the-go inspiration.

Recognising that today's busy families also need super quick and easy solutions for extra busy days, Annabel's award-winning retail food ranges for babies, toddlers and children can be discovered in the supermarket aisle. Inspired by her cookbook favourites, they have become household staples alongside her homemade recipes.

From kitchen table to global stage, Annabel uses her revolutionary food expertise and experience to campaign for better food standards. In 2006, Annabel received an MBE in the Queen's Birthday Honours for her outstanding work in the field of child nutrition, and she is also well recognised as a leading female entrepreneur and 'mumpreneur', spending time mentoring other parent-run businesses.

 @annabelkarmel

 @annabelkarmeluk

annabelkarmel.com

 @annabelkarmel